THE TRURO BEAR
AND OTHER ADVENTURES

The Truro Bear
and Other Adventures

POEMS AND ESSAYS

Mary Oliver

BEACON PRESS

BOSTON

Beacon Press
25 Beacon Street
Boston, Massachusetts 02108-2892
www.beacon.org

Beacon Press books
are published under the auspices of
the Unitarian Universalist Association of Congregations.

This book is printed on acid-free paper that meets the uncoated paper ANSI/NISO
specifications for permanence as revised in 1992.

Library of Congress Cataloging-in-Publication Data

Oliver, Mary
The truro bear and other adventures : poems and essays / Mary Oliver.
p. cm.
Includes bibliographical references and index.
ISBN-13: 978-0-8070-6884-7 (acid-free paper)
ISBN-10: 0-8070-6884-5 (acid-free paper) 1. Animals—Poetry. I. Title.

PS3565.L5T78 2008
811'.54—dc22 2008015400

POETRY
No Voyage and Other Poems
The River Styx, Ohio, and Other Poems
Twelve Moons
American Primitive
Dream Work
House of Light
New and Selected Poems Volume One
White Pine
West Wind
The Leaf and the Cloud
What Do We Know
Owls and Other Fantasies
Why I Wake Early
Blue Iris
New and Selected Poems Volume Two
Thirst
Red Bird

CHAPBOOKS AND SPECIAL EDITIONS
The Night Traveler
Sleeping in the Forest
Provincetown
Wild Geese (UK Edition)

PROSE
A Poetry Handbook
Blue Pastures
Rules for the Dance
Winter Hours
Long Life
Our World (with photographs by Molly Malone Cook)

CONTENTS

Truth is always veiled in a certain mystery.

Fabre, *The Life of the Fly*

On thy wondrous works I will meditate.

Psalm 145

The Chance to Love Everything

All summer I made friends
with the creatures nearby—
they flowed through the fields
and under the tent walls,
or padded through the door,
grinning through their many teeth,
looking for seeds,
suet, sugar; muttering and humming,
opening the breadbox, happiest when
there was milk and music. But once
in the night I heard a sound
outside the door, the canvas
bulged slightly—something
was pressing inward at eye level.
I watched, trembling, sure I had heard
the click of claws, the smack of lips
outside my gauzy house—
I imagined the red eyes,
the broad tongue, the enormous lap.
Would it be friendly too?
Fear defeated me. And yet,
not in faith and not in madness
but with the courage I thought
my dream deserved,

I stepped outside. It was gone.
Then I whirled at the sound of some
shambling tonnage.
Did I see a black haunch slipping
back through the trees? Did I see
the moonlight shining on it?
Did I actually reach out my arms
toward it, toward paradise falling, like
the fading of the dearest, wildest hope—
the dark heart of the story that is all
the reason for its telling?

The Gesture

On the dog's ear, a scrap of filmy stuff
    turns out to be
a walking stick, that jade insect, this one scarcely sprung
    from the pod of the nest,
not an inch long. I could just see
the eyes, elbows, feet nimble under the long shanks.
    I could not imagine it could live
in the brisk world, or where it would live, or how. But
    I took it
outside and held it up to the red oak that rises
    ninety feet into the air, and it lifted its forward-most
        pair of arms
with what in anything worth thinking about would have seemed
    a graceful and glad gesture; it caught
onto the bark, it hung on; it rested; it began to climb.

Porcupine

Where
the porcupine is
I don't
know but I hope

it's high
up on some pine
bough in some
thick tree, maybe

on the other side
of the swamp.
The dogs have come
running back, one of them

with a single quill
in his moist nose.
He's laughing,
not knowing what he has

almost done
to himself.
For years I have wanted to see
that slow rambler,

that thornbush.
I think, what love does to us
is a Gordian knot,
it's that complicated.

I hug the dogs
and their good luck,
and put on their leashes.
So dazzling she must be—

a plump, dark lady
wearing a gown of nails—
white teeth tearing skin
from the thick tree.

Toad

I was walking by. He was sitting there.

It was full morning, so the heat was heavy on his sand-colored head and his webbed feet. I squatted beside him, at the edge of the path. He didn't move.

I began to talk. I talked about summer, and about time. The pleasures of eating, the terrors of the night. About this cup we call a life. About happiness. And how good it feels, the heat of the sun between the shoulder blades.

He looked neither up nor down, which didn't necessarily mean he was either afraid or asleep. I felt his energy, stored under his tongue perhaps, and behind his bulging eyes.

I talked about how the world seems to me, five feet tall, the blue sky all around my head. I said, I wondered how it seemed to him, down there, intimate with the dust.

He might have been Buddha—did not move, blink, or frown, not a tear fell from those gold-rimmed eyes as the refined anguish of language passed over him.

One Hundred White-sided Dolphins on a Summer Day

1.

Fat,
black, slick,
galloping in the pitch
of the waves, in the pearly

fields of the sea,
they leap toward us,
they rise, sparkling, and vanish, and rise sparkling,
they breathe little clouds of mist, they lift perpetual smiles,

they slap their tails on the waves, grandmothers and grandfathers
enjoying the old jokes,
they circle around us,
they swim with us—

2.

a hundred white-sided dolphins
on a summer day,
each one, as God himself
could not appear more acceptable

a hundred times,
in a body blue and black threading through
the sea foam,
and lifting himself up from the opened

tents of the waves on his fishtail,
to look
with the moon of his eye
into my heart,

3.

and find there
pure, sudden, steep, sharp, painful
gratitude
that falls—

I don't know—either
unbearable tons
or the pale, bearable hand
of salvation

on my neck,
lifting me
from the boat's plain plank seat
into the world's

4.

unspeakable kindness.
It is my sixty-third summer on earth
and, for a moment, I have almost vanished
into the body of the dolphin,

into the moon-eye of God,
into the white fan that lies at the bottom of the sea
with everything
that ever was, or ever will be,

supple, wild, rising on flank or fishtail—
singing or whistling or breathing damply through blowhole
at top of head. Then, in our little boat, the dolphins suddenly gone,
we sailed on through the brisk, cheerful day.

The Kitten

More amazed than anything
I took the perfectly black
stillborn kitten
with the one large eye
in the center of its small forehead
from the house cat's bed
and buried it in a field
behind the house.

I suppose I could have given it
to a museum,
I could have called the local
newspaper.

But instead I took it out into the field
and opened the earth
and put it back
saying, it was real,
saying, life is infinitely inventive,
saying, what other amazements
lie in the dark seed of the earth, yes,

I think I did right to go out alone
and give it back peacefully, and cover the place
with the reckless blossoms of weeds.

Ghosts

1.

Have you noticed?

2.

Where so many millions of powerful bawling beasts
lay down on the earth and died
it's hard to tell now
what's bone, and what merely
was once.

The golden eagle, for instance,
has a bit of heaviness in him;
moreover the huge barns
seem ready, sometimes, to ramble off
toward deeper grass.

3.

1805
near the Bitterroot Mountains:
a man named Lewis kneels down
on the prairie watching

a sparrow's nest cleverly concealed in the wild hyssop
and lined with buffalo hair. The chicks,
not more than a day hatched, lean
quietly into the thick wool as if
content, after all,
to have left the perfect world and fallen,
helpless and blind
into the flowered fields and the perils
of this one.

4.

In the book of the earth it is written:
nothing can die.

In the book of the Sioux it is written:
they have gone away into the earth to hide.
Nothing will coax them out again
but the people dancing.

5.

Said the old-timers:
the tongue
is the sweetest meat.

Passengers shooting from train windows
could hardly miss, they were
that many.

Afterward the carcasses
stank unbelievably, and sang with flies, ribboned
with slopes of white fat,
black ropes of blood—hellhunks
in the prairie heat.

6.

Have you noticed? how the rain
falls soft as the fall
of moccasins. *Have you noticed?*
how the immense circles still,
stubbornly, after a hundred years,
mark the grass where the rich droppings
from the roaring bulls
fell to the earth as the herd stood
day after day, moon after moon
in their tribal circle, outwaiting
the packs of yellow-eyed wolves that are also
have you noticed? gone now.

7.

Once only, and then in a dream,
I watched while, secretly
and with the tenderness of any caring woman,
a cow gave birth
to a red calf, tongued him dry and nursed him

in a warm corner
of the clear night
in the fragrant grass
in the wild domains
of the prairie spring, and I asked them,
in my dream I knelt down and asked them
to make room for me.

Carrying the Snake to the Garden

In the cellar
was the smallest snake
I have ever seen.
It coiled itself
in a corner
and watched me
with eyes
like two little stars
set into coal,
and a tail
that quivered.
One step
of my foot
and it fled
like a running shoelace,
but a scoop of the wrist
and I had it
in my hand.
I was sorry
for the fear,
so I hurried
upstairs and out the kitchen door
to the warm grass
and the sunlight
and the garden.

It turned and turned
in my hand
but when I put it down
it didn't move.
I thought
it was going to flow
up my leg
and into my pocket.
I thought, for a moment,
as it lifted its face,
it was going to sing.

And then it was gone.

The Opossum

Beauty of fox, lemur, panther,
aardvark, thunder-worm, condor,

the quagga, the puffer, the kudu,
and this: the opossum

with her babies hanging on, gray lumps
all around the scaly tail

that was bent over her back, like a sailboat's boom,
for the very small and oh! almost human baby-fingers

to cling to. At first I thought
it was some pitiful broken thing

lumping along over the scrubby leaves,
and then I saw the brown dog-softness of her long-lashed eyes

as, swiftly, with that wobbling burden of life upon her,
she ran.

This Is the One

The bear
  who shuffles
    over the hillsides
      filling himself

with berries
  until his tongue is purple
    (which, remember, is
      a royal color)—

the bear
  who circles the cabin,
    who will not steal the honey,
      who will not rifle the knapsack

of the sleeping camper—
  the one
    who sits by himself
      by the river,

who sings to himself
  the secret song
    no one has ever heard—
      the bear

who yawns
   with the cavernous mouth
    of a shaggy god—
      who, when he sees me

is solidly silent
   and rises
    on the mass of his legs,
      disdainful and free

as anything on earth
   could ever be—
    this is the bear
      I want to see.

⋑ At Herring Cove

The edge of the sea shines and glimmers. The tide rises and falls, on ordinary not on stormy days, about nine feet. The beach here is composed of sand and glacial drift; the many-colored pebbles of this drift have been well rounded by the water's unceasing, manipulative, glassy touch. In addition, all sorts of objects are carried here by the currents, by the galloping waves, and left as the sea on the outgoing tide tumbles back.

From one tide to the next, and from one year to the next, what do I find here?

Grapefruit, and orange peel, and onion sacks from the fishing boats; balloons of all colors, with ribbons dangling; beer cans, soft drink cans, plastic bags, plastic bottles, plastic bottle caps, feminine hygiene by-products, a few summers ago several hypodermic needles, the odd glove and the odd shoe, plastic glasses, old cigarette lighters, mustard bottles, plastic containers still holding the decomposing bodies of baitfish; fishhooks rusty or still shining, coils of fishline; balls of fishline, one with a razor-billed auk in a death-grip.

Sea clams, razor clams, mussels holding on with their long beards to stones or each other; a very occasional old oyster and quahog shell; other shells in varying degrees of whiteness: drills, whelks, jingles, slippers, periwinkles, moon snails. Bones of fish, bodies of fish and of skates, pipefish, goosefish, jellyfish, dogfish, starfish, sand dabs; blues or parts of blues or the pink, satiny guts of blues; sand eels in the blackened seaweed, silver, and spackled with salt.

Dead harbor seal, dead gull, dead merganser, dead gannet

with tiny ivory-colored lice crawling over its snowy head and around its aster-blue eyes. Dead dovekie in winter.

Once, on a summer morning at exact low tide, the skull of a dolphin at the edge of the water. Later the flanged backbone, tail bones, hip bones slide onto the sand and return no more to the gardens of the sea.

One set of car keys. One quarter, green and salt-pocked.

Egg case of the left-handed whelk, black egg cases of skates; sea lace, the sandy nests of the moon snail, not one without its break in the circle; once, after a windy night, a drenched sea mouse.

More gorgeous than anything the mind of man has yet or ever will imagine, a moth, *Hyalophora cecropia,* in the first morning of its long death. I think of Thoreau's description of one he found in the Concord woods: "it looked like a young emperor just donning the most splendid robes that ever emperor wore. . . ." The wings are six inches across, and no part of them is without an extraordinary elaboration of design—swirls, circles, and lines, brief and shaped like lightning. Upon its taut understructure, the wings are powdery and hairy, like the finest fur closely shorn. White and cream and black, and a silver-blue, wine red and rust red, a light brown here and a darker brown there and still a deeper brown elsewhere, not to speak of the snowy white of the body's cylinder, and the stripes of the body, and the red fringe of the body, and the rust-colored legs, and the black plumes of the antennae. Once it was the hungry green worm. Then it flew, through the bottleneck of the deepest sleep, through the nets of the wind, into the warm field. And now it is the bright trash of the past, its emptiness perfect, and terrible.

Coyote in the Dark, Coyotes Remembered

The darkest thing
met me in the dark.
It was only a face
and a brace of teeth
that held no words,
though I felt a salty breath
sighing in my direction.
Once, in an autumn that is long gone,
I was down on my knees
in the cranberry bog
and heard, in that lonely place,
two voices coming down the hill,
and I was thrilled
to be granted this secret,
that the coyotes, walking together
can talk together,
for I thought, what else could it be?
And even though what emerged
were two young women, two-legged for sure
and not at all aware of me,
their nimble, young women tongues
telling and answering,
and though I knew
I had believed something probably not true,
yet it was wonderful

to have believed it.
And it has stayed with me
as a present once given is forever given.
Easy and happy they sounded,
those two maidens of the wilderness
from which we have—
who knows to what furious, pitiful extent—
banished ourselves.

Turtle

Now I see it—
it nudges with its bulldog head
the slippery stems of the lilies, making them tremble;
and now it noses along in the wake of the little brown teal

who is leading her soft children
from one side of the pond to the other; she keeps
close to the edge
and they follow closely, the good children—

the tender children,
the sweet children, dangling their pretty feet
into the darkness.
And now will come—I can count on it—the murky splash,

the certain victory
of that pink and gassy mouth, and the frantic
circling of the hen while the rest of the chicks
flare away over the water and into the reeds, and my heart

will be most mournful
on their account. But, listen,
what's important?
Nothing's important

except that the great and cruel mystery of the world,
of which this is a part,
not be denied. Once,
I happened to see, on a city street, in summer,

a dusty, fouled turtle plodding along—
a snapper—
broken out I suppose from some backyard cage—
and I knew what I had to do—

I looked it right in the eyes, and I caught it—
I put it, like a small mountain range,
into a knapsack, and I took it out
of the city, and I let it

down into the dark pond, into
the cool water,
and the light of the lilies,
to live.

The Other Kingdoms

Consider the other kingdoms. The
trees, for example, with their mellow-sounding
titles: oak, aspen, willow.
Or the snow, for which the peoples of the north
have dozens of words to describe its
different arrivals. Or the creatures, with their
thick fur, their shy and wordless gaze. Their
infallible sense of what their lives
are meant to be. Thus the world
grows rich, grows wild, and you too,
grow rich, grow sweetly wild, as you too
were born to be.

Swimming with Otter

I am watching otter, how he
    plays in the water, how he
        displays brave underside to the
            wave-washings, how he

breathes in descent trailing sudden
    strings of pearls that tell
        almost, but never quite, where he is
            apt to rise—how he is

gone, gone, so long I despair of him, then he
    trims, wetly, up the far shore and if he
        looks back he is surely
            laughing. I too have taken

my self into this
    summer lake, where the leaves of the trees
        almost touch, where peace comes
            in the generosity of water, and I have

reached out into the loveliness and I have
    floated on my flat back to think out
        a poem or two, not by any means fluid but,
            dear God, as you have made me, my only quickness.

Black Snake

I startled a young black snake: he
flew over the grass and hid his face

under a leaf, the rest of him in plain sight.
Little brother, often I've done the same.

Five A.M. in the Pinewoods

I'd seen
their hoofprints in the deep
needles and knew
they ended the long night

under the pines, walking
like two mute
and beautiful women toward
the deeper woods, so I

got up in the dark and
went there. They came
slowly down the hill
and looked at me sitting under

the blue trees, shyly
they stepped
closer and stared
from under their thick lashes and even

nibbled some damp
tassels of weeds. This
is not a poem about a dream,
though it could be.

This is a poem about the world
that is ours, or could be.
Finally
one of them—I swear it!—

would have come to my arms.
But the other
stamped sharp hoof in the
pine needles like

the tap of sanity,
and they went off together through
the trees. When I woke
I was alone,

I was thinking:
so this is how you swim inward,
so this is how you flow outward,
so this is how you pray.

Humpbacks

There is, all around us,
this country
of original fire.

You know what I mean.

The sky, after all, stops at nothing, so something
    has to be holding
our bodies
in its rich and timeless stables or else
we would fly away.

∞

Off Stellwagen
off the Cape,
the humpbacks rise. Carrying their tonnage
    of barnacles and joy
they leap through the water, they nuzzle back under it
like children
at play.

∞

They sing, too.
And not for any reason
you can't imagine.

❧

Three of them
rise to the surface near the bow of the boat,
then dive
deeply, their huge scarred flukes
tipped to the air.

We wait, not knowing
just where it will happen; suddenly
they smash through the surface, someone begins
shouting for joy and you realize
it is yourself as they surge
upward and you see for the first time
how huge they are, as they breach,
and dive, and breach again
through the shining blue flowers
of the split water and you see them
for some unbelievable
part of a moment against the sky—
like nothing you've ever imagined—
like the myth of the fifth morning galloping
out of darkness, pouring
heavenward, spinning; then

*

they crash back under those black silks
and we all fall back
together into that wet fire, you
know what I mean.

*

I know a captain who has seen them
playing with seaweed, swimming
through the green islands, tossing
the slippery branches into the air.

I know a whale that will come to the boat whenever
she can, and nudge it gently along the bow
with her long flipper.

I know several lives worth living.

*

Listen, whatever it is you try
to do with your life, nothing will ever dazzle you
like the dreams of your body,

its spirit
longing to fly while the dead-weight bones

toss their dark mane and hurry
back into the fields of glittering fire

where everything,
even the great whale,
throbs with song.

Moles

Under the leaves, under
the first loose
levels of earth
they're there—quick
as beetles, blind
as bats, shy
as hares but seen
less than these—
traveling
among the pale girders
of appleroot,
rockshelf, nests
of insects and black
pastures of bulbs
peppery and packed full
of the sweetest food:
spring flowers.
Field after field
you can see the traceries
of their long
lonely walks, then
the rains blur
even this frail
hint of them—
so excitable,

so plush,
so willing to continue
generation after generation
accomplishing nothing
but their brief physical lives
as they live and die,
pushing and shoving
with their stubborn muzzles against
the whole earth,
finding it
delicious.

The Snow Cricket

Just beyond the leaves and the white faces
of the lilies,
I saw the wings
of the green snow cricket

as it went flying
from vine to vine,
searching, then finding a shadowed place in which
to sit and sing—

and by singing I mean, in this instance,
not just the work of the little mouth-cave,
but of every enfoldment of the body—
a singing that has no words

or a single bar of music
or anything more, in fact, than one repeated
rippling phrase
built of loneliness

and its consequences: longing
and hope.
Pale and humped,
the snow cricket sat all evening

in a leafy hut, in the honeysuckle.
It was trembling
with the force
of its crying out,

and in truth I couldn't wait to see if another would come to it
for fear that it wouldn't,
and I wouldn't be able to bear it.
I wished it good luck, with all my heart,

and went back over the lawn, to where the lilies were standing
on their calm, cob feet,
each in the ease
of a single, waxy body

breathing contentedly in the chill night air;
and I swear I pitied them, as I looked down
into the theater of their perfect faces—
that frozen, bottomless glare.

Whelks

Here are the perfect
fans of the scallops,
quahogs, and weedy mussels
still holding their orange fruit—
and here are the whelks—
whirlwinds,
each the size of a fist,
but always cracked and broken—
clearly they have been traveling
under the sky-blue waves
for a long time.
All my life
I have been restless—
I have felt there is something
more wonderful than gloss—
than wholeness—
than staying at home.
I have not been sure what it is.
But every morning on the wide shore
I pass what is perfect and shining
to look for the whelks, whose edges
have rubbed so long against the world
they have snapped and crumbled—
they have almost vanished,
with the last relinquishing

of their unrepeatable energy,
back into everything else.
When I find one
I hold it in my hand,
I look out over that shaking fire,
I shut my eyes. Not often,
but now and again there's a moment
when the heart cries aloud:
yes, I am willing to be
that wild darkness,
that long, blue body of light.

A Meeting

She steps into the dark swamp
where the long wait ends.

The secret slippery package
drops to the weeds.

She leans her long neck and tongues it
between breaths slack with exhaustion

and after a while it rises and becomes a creature
like her, but much smaller.

So now there are two. And they walk together
like a dream under the trees.

In early June, at the edge of a field
thick with pink and yellow flowers

I meet them.
I can only stare.

She is the most beautiful woman
I have ever seen.

Her child leaps among the flowers,
the blue of the sky falls over me

like silk, the flowers burn, and I want
to live my life all over again, to begin again,

to be utterly
wild.

The Gift

After the wind-bruised sea
  furrowed itself back
    into folds of blue, I found
    in the black wrack

a shell called the Neptune—
  tawny and white,
    spherical,
      with a tail

and a tower
  and a dark door,
    and all of it
      no larger

than my fist.
  It looked, you might say,
    very expensive.
      I thought of its travels

in the Atlantic's
  wind-pounded bowl
    and wondered
      that it was still intact.

Ah yes, there was
　　that door
　　　　that held only the eventual, inevitable
　　　　　　emptiness.

There's that—there's always that.
　　Still, what a house
　　　　to leave behind!
　　　　　　I held it

like the wisest of books
　　and imagined
　　　　its travels toward my hand.
　　　　　　And now, your hand.

The Truro Bear

There's a bear in the Truro woods.
People have seen it—three or four,
or two, or one. I think
of the thickness of the serious woods
around the dark bowls of the Truro ponds;
I think of the blueberry fields, the blackberry tangles,
the cranberry bogs. And the sky
with its new moon, its familiar star-trails,
burns down like a brand-new heaven,
while everywhere I look on the scratchy hillsides
shadows seem to grow shoulders. Surely
a beast might be clever, be lucky, move quietly
through the woods for years, learning to stay away
from roads and houses. Common sense mutters:
it can't be true, it must be somebody's
runaway dog. But the seed
has been planted, and when has happiness ever
required much evidence to begin
its leaf-green breathing?

Alligator Poem

I knelt down
at the edge of the water,
and if the white birds standing
in the tops of the trees whistled any warning
I didn't understand,
I drank up to the very moment it came
crashing toward me,
its tail flailing
like a bundle of swords,
slashing the grass,
and the inside of its cradle-shaped mouth
gaping,
and rimmed with teeth—
and that's how I almost died
of foolishness
in beautiful Florida.
But I didn't.
I leaped aside, and fell,
and it streamed past me, crushing everything in its path
as it swept down to the water
and threw itself in,
and, in the end,
this isn't a poem about foolishness
but about how I rose from the ground
and saw the world as if for the second time,

turning its back
  with every tide on the past,
    leaving the shore littered
      every morning

with more ornaments of death—
  what a pearly rubble
    from which to choose a house
      like a white flower—

and what a rebellion
  to leap into it
    and hold on,
      connecting everything,

the past to the future—
  which is of course the miracle—
    which is the only argument there is
      against the sea.

Hannah's Children

They will come in their own time,
Probably in the black
Funnel of the night,
And probably in secret—
No one will see
Their marvelous coming
But the other goats,
And Maple the pony.

Now, on the evening
Of the last counted day,
We latch the stable door.
As the white moon rises
She settles to her knees.

Her curious yellow eyes—
Old as the stones
Of Greece, of the mountains
That were born with the world—
Look at us in friendship,
And then look away,

Inward. Inward
To the sacred groves.

Pipefish

In the green
  and purple weeds
    called *Zostera,* loosely
      swinging in the shallows,

I waded, I reached
  my hands
    in that most human
      of gestures—to find,

to see,
  to hold whatever it is
    that's there—
      and what came up

wasn't much
  but it glittered
    and struggled,
      it had eyes, and a body

like a wand,
  it had pouting lips.
    No longer,
      all of it,

than any of my fingers,
   it wanted
      away from my strangeness,
         it wanted

to go back
   into that waving forest
      so quick and wet.
         I forget

when this happened,
   how many years ago
      I opened my hands—
         like a promise

I would keep my whole life,
   and have—
      and let it go.
         I tell you this

in case you have yet to wade
   into the green
      and purple shallows
         where the diminutive

pipefish
   wants to go on living.
      I tell you this
         against everything you are—

your human heart,
   your hands passing over the world,
      gathering and closing,
         so dry and slow.

This Too

There was the body of the fawn, in the leaves,
    under the tall oaks.
There was the face, the succulent mouth,
    the pink, extruded tongue.
There were the eyes.
There was its dark dress, half pulled off.
There were its little hooves.
There was the smell of change, which was
    stink.
There was my dog's nose, reading the silence
    like a book.
No one spoke, not the Creator, not the Preserver,
    not the Destroyer.
There was the sound of wind in the leaves,
    in the tall oaks.
There was the terrible excitement
    of the flies.

❧ Swoon

In a corner of the stairwell of this rented house a most astonishing
adventure is going on. It is only the household of a common spi-
der,* a small, rather chaotic web half in shadow. Yet it burgeons
with the ambition of a throne. She—for it is the female that is
always in sight—has produced six egg sacs, and from three of
them, so far, an uncountable number of progeny have spilled.
Spilled is precisely the word, for the size and the motions of these
newborns are so meager that they appear at first utterly lifeless, as
though the hour of beginning had come and would not be
deferred, and thrust them out, with or without their will, to cling
in a dark skein in the tangled threads.

I am less precise about the timing of these events than I would
like. While I was quick to notice the spider and her web, I was
slow to write down the happenings as they occurred, a concor-
dance I now wish I had. It was so casual at first, I was sure that
something—probably a careless motion on my part—would
demolish or tear the web and remove the spider from sight. But it
did not happen.

I began to watch her in October, and it's fair to say that, being
a poor sleeper especially when away from home, I have watched
her quite as much during the night as during the day.

Now it is early December.

I am extremely careful as I descend or ascend the stairs.

Perhaps when I pass by she senses my heft and shadow. But
she floats on her strings and does not move. Nor, I think, would

---

*Probably *Theridium tepidariorum.*

she flee easily from any intrusion. Her egg sacs, all of them, are hanging near her, in an archipelago, the oldest at the top and the newest at the bottom, and without question she is attached to them in some bond of cherishing. Often she lies with her face against the most recently constructed, touching it with her foremost set of limbs. And why should she not be fond of it? She made it from the materials of her own body—deft and plump she circled and circled what was originally a small package, and caused it to grow larger as the thread flowed from her body. She wrapped and wrapped until, now, the sac sways with the others in the threads of the web, not round exactly, but like a Lilliputian gas balloon, pulled slightly along the vertical.

And still she fusses, pats it and circles it, as though coming to a judgment; then pats some more, or dozes, still touching it. Finally, she withdraws her sets of legs, curls them, almost as if in a swoon, or a death, and hangs, motionless, for a full half day. She seems to sleep.

The male spider comes and goes. Every third or fourth day I catch sight of him lurking at the edge of the web. What he eats I cannot guess, for the treasures of the web—which do not come, sometimes, for many days—are to all evidence for the female only. Whether she refuses to offer him a place at her table, or whether he has no need of it, I do not know. He is a dapper spider; being male and no spinner, he lacks the necessity of the pouch-like body in which to store the materials from which comes the bold and seemingly endless thread. He is therefore free to be of another nature altogether—small, and shy, and quick.

Twice while I have been watching, when the egg sacs have been in the unseeable process of pouring the tiny, billeted spiders forth, he has been in the web. Perhaps, like some male cats, and other mammals also, he will take this arrival with ill humor and feast on a few of his own progeny.

I do not know.

Whenever I see him poised there and lean closer to him, he steps briskly backward, is instantly enfolded into darkness and gone from sight.

It is five A.M.

Good fortune has struck the web like an avalanche. A cricket—not the black, flat-bodied, northern sort I am used to, but a paler variety, with a humped, shrimp-like body and whip-like antennae and jumper's legs—has become enmeshed in the web.

This spider is not an orb weaver; that is, she does not build a net silken and organized and centered along a few strong cables. No, her web is a poor thing. It is flung forth, ungloriously, only a few inches above the cellar floor. What is visible is in a wild disorder. Nevertheless, it functions; it holds, now, the six egg cases and the cricket, which struggles in a sort of sling of webbing.

The spider now is never still. She descends to the cricket again and again, then hastens away and hangs a short distance above. Though it is almost impossible to see, a fine line follows her, jetting from her spinneret; as she moves, she is wrapping the cricket. Soon the threads thicken; the cricket is bound with visible threads at the ankles, which keep it from tearing loose with the strength of the huge back legs. How does the spider know what it knows? Little by little the cricket's long front limbs with their serrated edges, flung in an outward gesture from its body, are also being wrapped. Soon the cricket's efforts to free itself are only occasional—a few yawings toward push or pull—then it is motionless.

All this has taken an hour.

There has been nothing consumable in the web for more than a week, during which time the spider has made her sixth egg case and, presumably, before that, carried through some motions of romance with her consort, and produced the actual eggs. Her body during this week—I mean that dust-colored, sofa-button, bulbous part of her body so visible to our eyes—has shrunk to half its previous size.

Then, as I continued to watch, the spider began a curious and coordinated effort. She dropped to the cricket and with her foremost limbs, which are her longest, she touched its body. The response was an immediate lurching of cricket, also spider and web. Swiftly she turned—she was, in fact, beginning the motions of turning even as she reached forward and then, even before the cricket reacted, with her hindmost pair of limbs she *kicked* it. She did this over and over—descending, touching and turning, kicking—each of her kicks targeting the cricket's stretched-out back limbs. She did this perhaps twenty times. With every blow the cricket swung, then rocked back to motionlessness, the only signs of life a small, continual motion of the jointed mouth, and a faint bubbling therefrom.

As I watched, the spider wrapped its thread again around the cricket's ankles. Then, with terrible and exact precision, she moved toward an indentation of flesh just at the elbow joint of the cricket's left front limb—and to this soft place she dipped her mouth. But, yet again, at this touch, the cricket lurched. So she retreated, and waited, and then again, with an undivertable aim, descended to that elbow where, finally, with no reaction from the cricket, she was able for perhaps three minutes to place her small face. There, as I imagine it, she began to infuse her flesh-dissolving venom into the channels of the cricket's body. Intermittently the cricket still moved, so this procedure even yet required some stopping and restarting, but it was clearly an unretractable operation. At length, in twenty minutes perhaps, the cricket lay utterly quiescent; and then the spider moved, with the most gentle and certain of motions, to the cricket's head, its bronze, visor-like face, and there, again surely and with no hesitation, the spider positioned her body, her mouth once more at some chosen juncture, near throat, the spinal cord, the brain.

Now she might have been asleep as she lay, lover-like, alongside the cricket's body. Later—hours later—she moved down along its bronze chest, and there fed again. Slowly her shrunken body grew larger, then very large. And then it was night.

◦§

Early in the morning, the cricket was gone. As I learned from later examples, when the quiescent cricket was no more than a shell, she had cut it loose. It had dropped to the cellar floor, where any number of living crickets occasionally went leaping by. By any one of them it had been dragged away. Now the spider, engorged, was motionless. She slept with her limbs enfolded slightly—the same half clench of limbs one sees in the bodies of dead spiders—but this was the twilight rest, not the final one. This was the restoration, the interval, the sleep of the exhausted and the triumphant.

I have not yet described the mystery and enterprise for which she lives—the egg sacs and the young spiders. They emerge from their felt balloon and hang on threads near it: a fling, a nebula. Only by putting one's face very close, and waiting, and not breathing, can one actually see that the crowd is moving. It is motion not at all concerted or even definite but it is motion, and that, compared with no movement at all, is of course everything. And it grows. Perhaps the spiders feel upon the tender hairs of their bodies the cool, damp cellar air, and it is a lure. They want more. They want to find out things. The tiny limbs stretch and shuffle.

Little by little, one or two, then a dozen, begin to drift into a wider constellation—toward the floor or the stair wall—spreading outward even as the universe is said to be spreading toward the next adventure and the next, endlessly.

In six or seven days after their birth, the little spiders are gone. And my attention passes from that opened and shrunken pod to the next below it, which is still secretly ripening, in which the many minuscule bodies are still packed tightly together, like a single thing.

How do they get out of the egg sac? Do they tear it with their fragile limbs? Do they chew it with their unimaginably tiny mouths?

I do not know.

Nor do I know where they all go, though I can imagine the dispersal of thousands into the jaws of the pale, leaping crickets. Certainly only a few of them survive, or we would be awash upon their rippling exertions.

Only once in this space of time, after the bursting of three of the six pods, did I see what was clearly a young spider; many times its original birth size and still no larger than a pencil's point, it was crawling steadily away through a last hem of the mother web.

This is the moment in an essay when the news culminates and, subtly or bluntly, the moral appears. It is a music to be played with the lightest fingers. All the questions that the spider's curious life made me ask, I know I can find answered in some book of knowledge, of which there are many. But the palace of knowledge is different from the palace of discovery, in which I am, truly, a Copernicus. *The world is not what I thought, but different, and more! I have seen it with my own eyes!*

But a spider? Even that?

Even that.

Our time in this rented house was coming to an end. For days I considered what to do with the heroine of this story and her enterprise, or if I should do anything at all. The owners of the house were to return soon; no reason to think they would not immediately sweep her away. And, in fact, we had ordered a housecleaning directly following our departure. Should I attempt to remove her, therefore? And if so, to what place? To the dropping temperatures of the yard, where surely she could not last out the coming winter? To another basement corner? But would the crickets be there? Would the shy male spider find her? Could I move the egg sacs without harming them, and the web intact, to hold them?

Finally, I did nothing. I simply was not able to risk wrecking her world, and I could see no possible way I could move the whole kingdom. So I left her with the only thing I could—the certainty of a little more time. For our explicit and stern instructions to the cleaners were to scrub the house—but to stay out of this stairwell altogether.

How Turtles Come to Spend the Winter in the Aquarium, Then Are Flown South and Released Back Into the Sea

Somewhere down beach, in the morning, at water's edge, I found
   a sea turtle,
its huge head a smoldering apricot, its shell streaming with sea-
   weed,
its eyes closed, its flippers motionless.
When I bent down, it moved a little.
When I picked it up, it sighed.
Was it forty pounds, or fifty pounds, or a hundred?
Was it two miles back to the car?
We walked a little while, and then we rested, and then we walked on
I walked with my mouth open, my heart roared.
The eyes opened, I don't know what they thought.
Sometimes the flippers swam at the air.
Sometimes the eyes closed.
I couldn't walk anymore, and then I walked some more
while it turned into granite, or cement, but with that apricot-
   colored head,
that stillness, that Buddha-like patience, that cold-shocked
but slowly beating heart.
Finally, we reached the car.

◆⑤

The afternoon is the other part of this story.
Have you ever found something beautiful, and maybe just in
   time?
How such a challenge can fill you!
Jesus could walk over the water.
I had to walk ankle-deep in the sand, and I did it.
My bones didn't quite snap.

Come on in, and see me smile.
I probably won't stop for hours.
Already, in the warmth, the turtle has raised its head, is looking
   around.
Today, who could deny it, I am an important person.

The Poet Goes to Indiana

I'll tell you a half-dozen things
that happened to me
in Indiana
when I went that far west to teach.
You tell me if it was worth it.

I lived in the country
with my dog—
part of the bargain of coming.
And there was a pond
with fish from, I think, China.
I felt them sometimes against my feet.
Also, they crept out of the pond, along its edges,
to eat the grass.
I'm not lying.
And I saw coyotes,
two of them, at dawn, running over the seemingly
unenclosed fields.
And once a deer, but a buck, thick-necked, leaped
into the road just—oh, I mean just, in front of my car—
and we both made it home safe.
And once the blacksmith came to care for the four horses,
or the three horses that belonged to the owner of the house,
and I bargained with him, if I could catch the fourth,
he, too, would have hooves trimmed

for the Indiana winter,
and apples did it,
and a rope over the neck did it,
so I won something wonderful;
and there was, one morning,
an owl
flying, oh pale angel, into
the hay loft of a barn,
I see it still;
and there was once, oh wonderful,
a new horse in the pasture,
a tall, slim being—a neighbor was keeping him there—
and she put her face against my face,
put her muzzle, her nostrils, soft as violets,
against my mouth and my nose, and breathed me,
to see who I was,
a long quiet minute—minutes—
then she stamped feet and whisked tail
and danced deliciously into the grass away, and came back.
She was saying, so plainly, that I was good, or good enough.
Such a fine time I had teaching in Indiana.

The Summer Day

Who made the world?
Who made the swan, and the black bear?
Who made the grasshopper?
This grasshopper, I mean—
the one who has flung herself out of the grass,
the one who is eating sugar out of my hand,
who is moving her jaws back and forth instead of up and down—
who is gazing around with her enormous and complicated eyes.
Now she lifts her pale forearms and thoroughly washes her face.
Now she snaps her wings open, and floats away.
I don't know exactly what a prayer is.
I do know how to pay attention, how to fall down
into the grass, how to kneel down in the grass,
how to be idle and blessed, how to stroll through the fields,
which is what I have been doing all day.
Tell me, what else should I have done?
Doesn't everything die at last, and too soon?
Tell me, what is it you plan to do
with your one wild and precious life?

Mink

A mink,
    jointless as heat, was
tip-toeing along
    the edge of the creek,

which was still in its coat of snow,
    yet singing—I could hear it!—
the old song
    of brightness.

It was one of those places,
    turning and twisty,
that Ruskin might have painted, though
    he didn't. And there were trees
leaning this way and that,
    seed-beaded

buckthorn mostly, but at the moment
    no bird, the only voice
that of the covered water—like a long,
    unknotted thread, it kept
slipping through. The mink
    had a hunger in him

bigger than his shadow, which was gathered
    like a sheet of darkness under his
neat feet which were busy
    making dents in the snow. He sniffed
slowly and thoroughly in all
    four directions, as though

it was a prayer to the whole world, as far
    as he could capture its beautiful
smells—the iron of the air, the blood
    of necessity. Maybe, for him, even
the pink sun fading away to the edge
    of the world had a smell,

of roses, or of terror, who knows
    what his keen nose was
finding out. For me, it was the gift of the winter
    to see him. Once, like a hot, dark-brown pillar,
he stood up — and then he ran forward, and was gone.
    I stood awhile and then walked on

over the white snow: the terrible, gleaming
    loneliness. It took me, I suppose,
something like six more weeks to reach
    finally a patch of green, I paused so often
to be glad, and grateful, and even then carefully across
    the vast, deep woods I kept looking back.

THE PERCY POEMS

❧

Percy (One)

Our new dog, named for the beloved poet,
ate a book which unfortunately we had
   left unguarded.
Fortunately it was the *Bhagavad Gita,*
of which many copies are available.
Every day now, as Percy grows
into the beauty of his life, we touch
his wild, curly head and say,

"Oh, wisest of little dogs."

Percy (Two)

I have a little dog who likes to nap with me.
He climbs on my body and puts his face in my neck.
He is sweeter than soap.
He is more wonderful than a diamond necklace,
    which can't even bark.
I would like to take him to Kashmir and the Ukraine,
    and Jerusalem and Palestine and Iraq and Darfur,
that the sorrowing thousands might see his laughing mouth.
I would like to take him to Washington, right into
    the oval office
where Donald Rumsfeld would crawl out of the president's
    armpit
and kneel down on the carpet, and romp like a boy.

For once, for a moment, a rational man.

Little Dog's Rhapsody in the Night (Three)

He puts his cheek against mine
and makes small, expressive sounds.
And when I'm awake, or awake enough

he turns upside down, his four paws
    in the air
and his eyes dark and fervent.

Tell me you love me, he says.

Tell me again.

Could there be a sweeter arrangement? Over and over
he gets to ask it.
I get to tell.

Percy (Four)

I went to church.
I walked on the beach
and played with Percy.

I answered the phone
and paid the bills.
I did the laundry.

I spoke her name
a hundred times.

I knelt in the dark
and said some holy words.

I went downstairs,
I watered the flowers,
I fed Percy.

News of Percy (Five)

In the morning of his days he is in the afternoon of his life.
It's some news about kidneys, those bean-shaped necessities,
   of which, of his given two, he has one working, and
      that not well.

We named him for the poet, who died young, in the blue
   waters off Italy.
Maybe we should have named him William, since Wordsworth
   almost never died.

We must laugh a little at this rich and unequal world,
   so they say, so they say.
And let them keep saying it.

Percy and I are going out now, to the beach, to join
   his friends—
the afghan, the lab, the beautiful basset.
And let me go with good cheer in his company.
For though he is young he is beloved,
   he is all but famous as he runs
across the shining beach, that faces the sea.

Percy (Six)

You're like a little wild thing
that was never sent to school.
Sit, I say, and you jump up.
Come, I say, and you go galloping down the sand
to the nearest dead fish
with which you perfume your sweet neck.
It is summer.
How many summers does a little dog have?

Run, run, Percy.
This is our school.

Percy (Seven)

And now Percy is getting brazen.
Let's down the beach, baby, he says.
Let's shake it with a little barking.
Let's find dead things, and explore them,
by mouth, if possible.

Or maybe the leavings of Paul's horse (after which,
forgive me for mentioning it, he is fond of kissing).

Ah, this is the thing that comes to each of us.
The child grows up.
And, according to our own ideas, is practically asunder.

I understand it.
I struggle to celebrate.
I say, with a stiff upper lip familiar to many:

Just look at that curly-haired child now, he's his own man.

Percy and Books (Eight)

Percy does not like it when I read a book.
He puts his face over the top of it and moans.
He rolls his eyes, sometimes he sneezes.
The sun is up, he says, and the wind is down.
The tide is out and the neighbor's dogs are playing.
But Percy, I say. Ideas! The elegance of language!
The insights, the funniness, the beautiful stories
that rise and fall and turn into strength, or courage.

Books? says Percy. I ate one once, and it was enough.
Let's go.

Percy (Nine)

Your friend is coming I say
to Percy, and name a name

and he runs to the door, his
wide mouth in its laugh-shape,

and waves, since he has one, his tail.
Emerson, I am trying to live,

as you said we must, the examined life.
But there are days I wish

there was less in my head to examine,
not to speak of the busy heart. How

would it be to be Percy, I wonder, not
thinking, not weighing anything, just running forward.

I Ask Percy How I Should Live My Life
(Ten)

Love, love, love, says Percy.
And hurry as fast as you can
along the shining beach, or the rubble, or the dust.

Then, go to sleep.
Give up your body heat, your beating heart.
Then, trust.

Percy at His Bath, or, Ambivalence (Eleven)

Today Jill is cutting my snags and my curls.
My legs grow longer.
My tail gets brushed.
Then, the bath.

Mary has been reading a book about
a woman who made a secret journey
to Lhasa. She reads aloud to me the parts
about the village dogs, who are big and
fearless and full of bark. And, all
their lives, dirty. I am filled
with envy.

Then it's over and I am in my bed
as white as snow and soft and all
the sea salt gone. And over every part of me
an absurd but lovely fragrance.

Percy at Breakfast (Twelve)

Percy says, I've eaten and I'm still hungry.
So I say, what about toast? and offer him
    a dry corner.
Percy says, I like butter better.

Eggs then? I say. And we share a couple scrambled.

Good! says Percy. And then because he's polite sometimes,
    Thank you.

He turns to leave the room, then looks back
philosophically. I guess people just don't understand,
he says, how it is never to be not hungry.

Percy Speaks While I Am Doing Taxes
(Thirteen)

First of all, I do not want to be doing this.
Second of all, Percy does not want me
   to be doing this,
hanging over my desk like a besieged person
   with a dull pencil and innumerable lists
     of numbers.

Outside the water is blue, the sky is clear,
   the tide rising.
Percy, I say, this has to be done. This is
   essential. I'll be finished eventually.

Keep me in your thoughts, he replies. Just because
   I can't count to ten doesn't mean
I don't remember yesterday, or anticipate today.
   I give you one more hour, then we step out
into the beautiful, money-deaf gift of the world
   and run.

ACKNOWLEDGMENTS

"The Truro Bear" and "Hannah's Children" are from *Twelve Moons,* copyright © 1979 by Mary Oliver. Reprinted by permission of Little, Brown Book Group.

"The Chance to Love Everything," "The Kitten," "Ghosts," "Humpbacks," "Moles," and "A Meeting" are from *American Primitive* by Mary Oliver, copyright © 1983 by Mary Oliver. Reprinted by permission of Little, Brown Book Group.

"Turtle," "Five A.M. in the Pinewoods," "The Hermit Crab," "Pipefish," "How Turtles Come to Spend the Winter in the Aquarium, Then Are Flown South and Released Back Into the Sea," and "The Summer Day" are from *House of Light,* copyright © 1990 by Mary Oliver. Reprinted by permission of Beacon Press.

"The Gesture" is from *White Pine: Poems and Prose Poems,* copyright © 1992 by Mary Oliver. Reprinted by permission of Houghton Mifflin Harcourt Publishing Company.

"Porcupine" and "Toad" are from *White Pine: Poems and Prose Poems,* copyright © 1994 by Mary Oliver, reprinted by permission of Houghton Mifflin Harcourt Publishing Company.